DISCERNMENT

- A WAY OF LIFE -

The Upper Room Home of Prayer Community
Rosemary O'Toole CSJ, Editor

DISCERN
PRODUCTS

Copyright © 2014 by The Upper Room Home of Prayer
Ottawa, Ontario

All Bible quotations are from the Jerusalem Bible

Published by:
Discern Products
724 Parkdale Ave.
Ottawa, Ontario K1Y 1J6
info@discernproducts.com

For book orders including bulk orders, please contact
upperroom@sympatico.ca

Cover illustration by Judith Veeder
Interior photographs by Betty Ross

Library and Archives Canada Cataloguing in Publication
is available upon request

ISBN 978-09680061-4-6

Printed by Gauvin Press
Gatineau, Quebec

ABOUT THE AUTHORS

This Contemplative Discernment Process was studied, observed and practised at Lebh Shomea House of Prayer in South Texas where Rosemary O'Toole CSJ lived for three years (1981-84). Here she completed a program of tutored studies receiving a certificate of studies in the Theology of Christian Spirituality. In September 1984, she began the ministry of spiritual direction at The Upper Room Home of Prayer in Ottawa, Canada.

The directors at Lebh Shomea House of Prayer, Francis Kelly Nemeck, OMI and Marie Theresa Coombs, hermit, wrote the book, The Way of Spiritual Direction in 1985. It has been acclaimed as a modern day classic.

In 1989, with their permission and encouragement, Sister Rosemary began to offer a two year **Emmaus Program** for the facilitation of the gift of spiritual direction at The Upper Room Home of Prayer using their book as the primary textbook. After nine Emmaus Programs, several spiritual directors now contribute actively to the ministry.

This book, Discernment: A Way of Life was prepared by Betty Ross, Barbara Graham and Rosemary O'Toole CSJ to offer some genuine spiritual accompaniment in service to the mission of evangelization and to encourage growth in the Christian life.

This booklet is prepared for individuals or small group conversations. The Upper Room Home of Prayer community hopes the process described here will contribute to our readers understanding and practice of discernment in their daily life circumstances. For years, it has been a trustworthy guide for us in our personal lives and in our spiritual direction ministry.

CONTENTS

INTRODUCTION

How can I know what God wants for me? People who sincerely want to integrate their faith and daily living will encounter this question.

➤ **Big Decisions of Life**
- vocation, career, retirement, buying a house
- starting a new relationship, ending a relationship

➤ **New Directions in Life**
- choosing my school/college/university
- changing jobs, cities
- involvement in ministry; volunteer work
- empty nest syndrome: What do I do now with my life?

➤ **Areas of Personal Growth**
- relational challenges at home, at school, at work
- personal discontent, restlessness
- moral struggle, compulsive behavior
- set personal boundaries, anger management

➤ **Spiritual Growth**
- wanting a spiritual life/friends/community
- really searching for God and knowing my true self

- inner disquiet, aridity in prayer and daily life
- want inner peace
- desire deeper union with God
- sensing a perceived 'absence' of God
- devotional practice changing

These questions will be ongoing. They will ebb and flow with the many thresholds and stages of our life journey. Certainly when it comes to changes in lifestyle, choosing our life vocation and making important decisions, we want to know what God has to say to us on these matters. But how does that happen?

Discernment is the term we use for that process of clarifying and understanding God's will for us. The biblical meaning of discernment includes both detecting the origins of our inclinations, desires, inspirations and insights and evaluating the signs by which one might know if a given course of action or teaching seems to be of God or not. You might be asking yourself, "How do I know what and when I might be in need of this gift of discernment?" As many people experience, God often initiates change in unusual ways. Discernment anticipates change.

Some harbingers of change are:
- an inner restlessness
- an increased longing and desire for a life partner
- frustration with one's present situation
- dissatisfaction with material things and accomplishments

- a sense that I am not yet living my life fully
- 'something within' seems to be nudging me, prodding me forward, outside my current comfort zone
- undergoing inter-personal struggles
- deepening my relationship and sensing it's time for making a commitment
- working through some conflicting values
- spending time just yearning for God, for I-know-not-what
- some practical choice just needs to be made (house/job)
- someone close to me has a decision to make that will affect me also

Matters for discernment are often vague at first, and can present several options. They usually involve a more or less desirable preference. Life is complex. God often initiates a new direction with a hunch, a nudge, just to get our attention. Sometimes 'it' comes from within us, and sometimes, 'it' is an invitation from someone else. But we know we need to make a response. So, we seek clarity. That brings us to the need for discernment.

Pause and Reflect

Identify your 'discernment issue' as specifically as possible.

What's going on?

Who is involved?

Why is this issue important for you right now?

What life change are you considering?

Chapter 1

OPENING TO INNER WISDOM

"Wisdom is bright, and does not grow dim.
By those who love her she is readily seen,
and found by those who look for her.
Quick to anticipate those who desire her,
she makes herself known to them."
- Wisdom 6:12

Ignatius of Loyola, the founder of the Jesuit religious Order, called discernment, "finding God in all things." The habit of discernment is an attitude of listening to God in all of life. Many times throughout our lives, we have searched and prayed to know God's will for us. Like Mary, we too want to say "Let what you have said be done to me" (Lk. 1:38). But how can I be sure it is God speaking to me and not just my own voice in my head? We hear others speak of being called by God to take certain actions or knowing God's will for them, but we wonder: How will I know God's will for me?

Discernment is not just for the major decisions of our life. The greatest gift of discernment is that it becomes a way of life, an attitude of "listening and attending with the ear of the heart" to all that is happening. (St. Benedict) Over time and with awareness, the "ear of the heart" grows accustomed to recognizing, almost spontaneously, those movements that are drawing us into oneness with God, ourselves and all creation and those that tend to isolate us even from ourselves. Like the wise Solomon we pray:

> "Give your servant a heart to understand how to discern between good and evil, for who could govern this people of yours that is so great?" (1 Kings 3:10)

Discernment grows from the firm belief that God is actively and caringly involved with us in every moment of our lives, even the seemingly most mundane ones. Not only is God indwelling us, God's Spirit, Inner Wisdom, is guiding us to live an authentic expression of God's presence in each moment. We become who we truly are as we live in congruence with God and our true authentic self. Eventually we find ourselves moving more in unison with God's desires and plans and it becomes one simple loving presence: "I live now not with my own life but with the life of Christ who lives in me" (Gal. 2:20).

Discernment of spirits is the interpretation of what Ignatius of Loyola called the "motions of the soul." These interior movements consist of thoughts, imaginings, emotions, inclinations, desires, feelings, repulsions, and attractions. Spiritual discernment of spirits involves becoming sensitive to these movements, reflecting on them, and understanding where they come from and where they lead us.

The Biblical meaning of discernment includes both detecting the origins of our inclinations, desires, inspirations, and insights and evaluating the signs by which one might know if a given course of action seems to be of God or not.

Discernment is a gift, a charism of the Spirit. St. Paul names it specifically as one of the gifts of the Spirit given to certain members of the community for the good of the community. It is a personal gift but never a private gift. It's not about studying discernment or using a specific process to get it right. The core of discernment is praying that God enlighten and move us in the direction God wants and desires us to go.

> "Among the gifts of the Spirit scarcely one is of greater practical usefulness than the gift of discernment. This gift should be highly valued and frankly sought as being almost indispensable in these critical times. This gift will enable us to distinguish the chaff from the wheat and to divide the manifestations of the flesh from the operations of the Spirit."
>
> - A. W. Tozer

The very fact that a person is concerned about God's will is evidence of an active, developing, maturing faith life. Discernment is not something we copy and paste like a computer function into our lives as the need arises. Discernment arises out of an ongoing, developing life of prayer and religious practice. A maturing self-awareness, wholesome living and participation in a worshipping community stimulate the environmental conditions necessary for hearing and discerning God's Spirit.

Discernment is understanding the root causes that create surface problems.

Consider these things. A balanced life of prayer, work, study and leisure is a good pre-requisite for discerning God's will in our daily life situations. Many of our problems and struggles have origins in physical or emotional distress. Just note the difference a poor night's sleep has on one's outlook the following day. Prolonged stress can trigger relationship problems. Sometimes a holiday, or reading some recovery work, or sharing a meal with friends, brings deep relaxation.

> "Enjoy reasonable relaxation, at the proper time and with the right persons. The bow that is always taut will not be able to stand the strain without breaking."
> - J.P. Medaille, SJ, Maxim of Perfection, 13:8

If a person is sensing a need for a change, entertaining a new idea as God-inspired, he/she needs to check out the physical/psychological factors first. A troubling restlessness may be a result of poor sleep or nutrition habits or unresolved personal issues. A time of emotional suffering, such as grief or depression, may suggest taking up new projects or adventures or leaving a career and family commitments. Take your time with those major life changes. If the root cause is 'the dark night of the soul' then it manifests as an urgency to know and feel God's presence...that now mysteriously feels like the 'absence' of God. One's faith is being stretched and all of one's life seems enveloped by this aridity. All these factors will influence how one makes decisions, especially faith-based ones.

It is paramount to identify the presence of any 'root causes' in dealing with our surface problems. Are there physical, psychological, emotional and/or spiritual issues that need attention? God may indeed be using the life-stressor to initiate a new direction, but for good discernment, the other factors must be given due attention at the same time. You may need to consult your family doctor, a therapist, or/and a spiritual director if there are any medical or emotional problems requiring attention at the same time as you pray with your discernment question. God is working in and through all.

Discernment will be true to you and true to God. Trust that God's will for you will be good for you. Paul urges believers to "test and approve God's good and perfect will" (Romans 12:2). Trust that any call of God will be consistent with our true personhood - one's true self in union with God. God does not impose on people arbitrary directions that are contrary to their God-given nature, personality, temperament or gifts. Through careful discernment, you will come to see that God's direction will be a 'good fit' for you.

But a 'good fit' doesn't always mean an 'easy fit'. God's calls in our daily life situations can often involve risk and perhaps even invite major transitions. These decisions may even prove costly, fulfilling in your own self the words of Jesus: "Anyone who finds his life will lose it; anyone who loses his life for my sake will find it" (Mt. 10:39). The Spanish mystic, John of the Cross, confirms that deep, lasting satisfaction and peace is found only in doing God's will.

"Have only one desire throughout your life: to be, and to become, what God wants you to be, in nature, in grace, and in glory, for time and eternity."
- J.P. Medaille, SJ, Maxim of Perfection 10:6

Desire for God alone accelerates one's openness, co-operation and receptivity to whatever God's call is in any given situation. When we keep our attentiveness and focus on this 'in God alone is my peace' we seem to move along in our discernment process with more serenity and grace. In truth, our desire for God is actually a response of God's prior call for us and God's desire that we abide in intimate communion. Take courage and place your trust in God even now, in the 'not-knowing' your future decision. God IS leading and guiding your life and wants to reassure you with 'signs and fruits' that you will be able to recognize.

Love and freedom are the wonderful fruits of this discernment practice as it becomes a way of life. We can speak of a strong desire for knowing and understanding God's will in our lives, but this becomes greatly enhanced when we live continuously in the actual *experience* of God's love in our lives. Start now to cultivate a gratitude for all of God's works and gifts in your life. Believe in God's nearness and abiding presence within you. You are beautifully and wonderfully made. We are "created in the image and likeness of God," (Gen. 1:26) and God wants all of us to reach our full maturity.

The sense of freedom we are referring to here is an inner personal freedom which allows us to give God and God's will a central place in our lives. It is a freedom and detachment from all other things that would either prevent or hinder our attempts to focus on God. It is the central freedom that allows God to become and remain the central reality of our lives. It is a free and dependent attitude towards all of God's gifts so that we love them with a well-ordered love. We find God in them and we appreciate them as manifestations of God's will for us.

When we have allowed God to heal and free us (to some extent at least) of our selfishness, our disorders, our dysfunctions, and our inordinate attachments, the inner turmoil calms down and we are released from needless anxiety. Over time, this new interior freedom in God facilitates clearer discernment.

Pray this mantra:
Empty me. Fill me with your Great Love.

So, let us ponder this well. Our primary spiritual task is to facilitate growth into this freedom that brings forth such joy and peace. This is our call and challenge throughout the journey of life. We all have real lives. We have to cope with the demands and responsibilities of work and family. We may be facing financial and emotional struggles at home. We may be gripped by anxieties, fears and compulsions which preoccupy our emotional and spiritual energies. What a wonderful grace when we can "find God in all things." Yes, God speaks to us about these matters.

As we seek to grow and mature into whole persons... one day at a time... and learn to pursue wholesome patterns of living and relating, our sense of personal freedom in God and our true selves will emerge. This is just the way we evolve in spiritual genesis - moving always towards 'the more.' Stay the course. True peace is gift.

Pause and Reflect

What is a "surface problem" in your life now? Name it briefly, clearly, directly.

Jot down your understanding of the 'root causes'. Is there an area of imbalance for which you need to take immediate corrective action? Do you need to make an appointment with a physician, spiritual director or counselor?

Consider God's works and gifts in your life. Take a few moments to bask in these signs of God's love for you. Are you living in an awareness of this love?

Chapter 2

PREPARING YOUR HEART

"That is why I am going to lure her and lead her out into
the wilderness and speak to her heart...Here, I will betroth
you with integrity and justice, with tenderness and love.
I will betroth you to myself with faithfulness,
and you will come to know Yahweh."
- Hosea 2:16, 21

Discernment is ultimately about love. This contemplative approach to discernment calls forth an interior freedom. It is like falling in love; one is grasped by God's goodness. God is beholding us in love. We want to respond in love to the choices we make in our everyday living and relationships. It brings forth such good fruits and real happiness. While discernment is a special charismatic gift for some Christians, we are all called to grow in the dispositions of soul - qualities of heart - that will dispose us to receive this precious gift.

There are four pre-conditions necessary in persons so that the emergence of their spiritual direction can take place.

1. Solitary prayer

Daily prayer opens us to a loving encounter with God that allows us to face the truth of God and the truth of oneself. In our prayer we become willing to abandon ourselves to God's purifying and transforming love. Yes, in facing our inner poverty, we must be willing to undergo being stripped by God of our illusions, attachments, defenses and egocentricity. Do I have an awareness of my sinfulness? Can I acknowledge my need for healing and reconciliation?

"Yahweh is so good...in all that is right, he guides the humble and instructs the poor in his way" (Psalm 25:9).

Am I sincerely seeking to be aware of God's direction for my life? Do I desire to live "the sacrament of the present moment" as Jean-Pierre de Caussade, SJ (18th Century mystic) called it? Ultimately, it is when we recollect ourselves to the Divine Mystery that we can fully reap the ripened fruits of our faith. For, when the spirit consents to rest in God, to say and truly mean "Your will be done," (Mt. 6:10) then something wonderful happens. Alas, the divine action, infused with grace, does its part to enkindle awareness of God in the present moment.

Prayer 'wakes up' our awareness of being loved by God. Prayer fans into a flame the life of God within us. Yes, the Spirit is given to us and is indwelling every person at the deepest core of our being. Jesus calls us to "Abide in my love. Make your home in me as I make mine in you. Remain in My love" (Jn. 15:9).

Pray this mantra:
God with me. God within me. God beyond me.

- How have I benefited from periods of silent prayer?
- What struggles/joys do I encounter during my prayer?
- Do I listen to God in prayer? Or do I still talk too much?
- Do I realize I am loved by God? Really loved?
- Am I drawn to more silence? More solitude?

- Do I have an awareness of my sinfulness? And those aspects of human weakness/dysfunctional patterns?

2. Desire for the truth

The truth intensifies freedom and inner peace. The truth is often bitter medicine to swallow. Truth necessarily purges all that is untruthful. It uproots and detaches, corrects and reproves, often thrusting us in a way we would rather not go.

"You will learn the truth and the truth shall make you free" (Jn. 8:32). Am I honest, receptive and open to God's initiatives? Am I stubborn, resistant, obstinate and closed-minded? Some persons want only partial truths; so they compromise, rationalize, not wanting it to cost too much, or they slip into complacency.

There will often be a call to conversion within a discernment process. The voice of God speaks clearly in a pure heart. In order to discern God's will for our lives, we need to seek the truth and be willing to accept the challenge, questioning and confrontation that the truth brings. Soften my heart and let it ripen and be molded and fashioned in the loving Potter's hands.

Self-knowledge is needed in discernment. "Anyone who loses his life for my sake will find it" (Mt. 10:39). Throughout the process, there will necessarily be a feeling of dying to our 'small self', our 'false self.' Our wounded little ego-self sounds like, "I want what I want when I want it!" Our self-centeredness will be progressively purged throughout discernment.

Discernment opens us up to conversion, to REAL change, to becoming our bigger self, our true self - the person God made in his own likeness. God's Goodness and Great Love effect in us this transformation daily in all the little and big surrenders we make throughout our discernment process.

- Am I willing to change? To try new things?
- How do I let go control?
- Do I accept challenge, questioning, confrontation from trusted others? They may have some truth that will set me free.
- How receptive and open to God's ways am I really?
- Do I observe stubborn, resistant, obstinate and closed-minded attitudes in some aspects of my life?
- Is there a 'conversion call' nudging me in this situation?
- What if God is trying to set me free? Really free?
- Be aware of how harmony with 'the truth' feels within.

3. Openness to outcome

Often, we bring questions or decisions to God having already decided what the 'right' answer should be. In order to discern God's direction for our lives, we need to be open to the outcome, ready to say, "Let your will be done, not mine" (Lk. 22:42). This inner disposition can be difficult to achieve. However, the process of discernment itself, will affect in us a readiness and a necessity to abandon ourselves to the will of our all-loving God. It is necessary to have some objectivity in discernment. We need to be able to transcend our own personal preferences.

Discernment requires a prayerful consideration of every aspect of the matter in question, while remaining open to every possible solution or outcome. This openness to do whatever the Spirit reveals and then the courage to follow it in faith is the strength of good discernment.

Be aware that the principal obstacle to openness with respect to the outcome of a discernment process is usually a person's fixation on some particular way or result. This strong latching on to our own desire can blind us and deafen our listening to God, let alone anyone else! Just be mindful here… sometimes another person has an insight that enlarges my discernment. Sometimes, there is a way of looking at the same issue that comes only in time or upon the right set of outer circumstances. Many of us have seen discernment unfold like this over time.

- What ways have I discovered to let go control of my life and allow God to move me forward?
- Try this spiritual practice: Let go. Let be. Let flow.
- Can I identify my set ways, set patterns of thinking and being and doing that are obstacles to growth into 'the more?'

4. Willingness to wait in patience

Waiting is an important dimension of the discernment process. In God's time and in God's way, the direction will reveal itself. Patience enables us, while we are moving forward, to live fully in the present, to listen to God as he speaks in the here and now. Even though one may not comprehend how, the Spirit is nonetheless already guiding us to a clearer perception of the way forward.

A heart that is waiting patiently in eager expectancy will eventually come into the way of wisdom and will perceive the action of God and be capable of learning what the Spirit wants.

- Do I already perceive that this waiting in patience is freeing my mind and heart of useless mental clutter and anxiety about the direction?
- How am I learning to just live with my question? I trust that "one day the answer will just be there" – as an inner knowing. I will receive the grace to move forward in that new direction.
- Offer gratitude and acceptance throughout this process.

Ponder deeply…

Above all, trust in the slow work of God.
We are quite naturally impatient in everything
    to reach the end without delay.
We should like to skip the intermediate stages.
We are impatient of being on the way to
    something unknown, something new.
And yet it is the law of all progress
    that it is made by passing through
    some stages of instability –
    and that it may take a very long time.

And so I think it is with you;
    your ideas mature gradually - let them grow,
    let them shape themselves without undue haste.
Don't try to force them on,
    as though you could be today what time

(that is to say, grace and circumstances
acting on your own good will)
will make you tomorrow.

Only God could say what this new spirit
gradually forming within you will be.
Give our Lord the benefit of believing
that his hand is leading you,
and accept the anxiety of feeling yourself
in suspense and incomplete.

-Pierre Teilhard de Chardin, S.J. Hearts on
Fire, Praying with Jesuits, p. 58.

Pause and Reflect

How have these four pre-conditions helped you prepare your heart for receiving the gift of discernment?

Pray with this wonderfully wise spiritual maxim:

Never go ahead of grace
through imprudent eagerness
but await its moment in peace,
and when it comes to you,
follow it with great gentleness and courage.
Once you have obeyed,
take care lest complacency
rob you of the fruit of your obedience.

- *J.P. Medaille, SJ, Maxim of Perfection 6:9*

Chapter 3

PRAYING WITH YOUR QUESTION

"Eli then understood that it was the Lord
who was calling the boy, and he said to Samuel;
Go and lie down, and if someone calls say,
"Speak, Lord, your servant is listening."
- 1 Samuel 3:9

At this stage in your discernment process, it is vital to spend time in prayer, discovering and forming your specific question. We often start with a vague feeling that God is nudging us or calling us in a particular direction, or to do something different, but we don't know for sure what that is or might be. Often, the question changes or deepens as we pray with it. We need to bring a clearly formed, unambiguous question to our discernment.

> Your question should take the form of:
>
> **Is God calling me to _____?**

Name it as a clear, specific action or choice. You should be able to recognize the answer as a clear YES or NO. Do not ask either/or questions.

Examples of questions that are clear and specific:
- Is God calling me to apply for this university science course?
- Is God calling me to leave my pastoral care ministry?
- Is God calling me to a marriage commitment?

Examples of questions that are NOT clear and specific:
- Is God calling me to serve on the liturgy committee or the finance committee?
- Is God calling me to change?
- Is God calling me to sell my home or stay in my home?

Praying with your question

Ask God your SPECIFIC question during times of solitary prayer. Don't expect an answer in a particular time frame. Be faithful and persistent in your prayer. Does a Scripture passage surface into your consciousness that speaks to your present situation? If so, be with it for expanded insight and 'direction' on your problem/question.

It's about simple awareness of inner stirrings without mental analysis. Let the mind be still and try not to engage with logic and reasons and explanations. It just IS there … as it is … and let the 'stirrings' be.

We are not our thoughts, our emotions, or our bodily impulses. We are invited to choose from our soul Centre, where God dwells. "Remain in my love" (Jn. 15.9).

As contemplative awareness deepens over time you will be able to recognize the different origins of these feelings and act with more wisdom and insight. Be patient as you become more familiar with the stirrings of the Spirit within you.

Discernment must begin with paying attention to our feelings and these interior movements.

As you are praying with your SPECIFIC question be aware of your feelings. These feelings are the raw material for insight into your discernment question. They are essential to our spiritual life and to the discovery of God's will. Name your feelings as they arise. Claim them (do not repress them). The intellect can then judge the source and the validity of these feelings.

Is the source physical, psychological, spiritual?

For example, as you continue praying with your question …you realize that your spirit seems to grow weary and discouraged. You are lacking energy and enthusiasm for life. These feelings could be an indication of a physical or chronic illness, or they could be a psychological manifestation of a low-grade depression or a consequence of addictive behaviours. And yes indeed, they could be a sign of undergoing a spiritual dark night of the senses.

Thus, you can see how important it is that our feelings must be understood and evaluated to distinguish the Holy Spirit from the ego/false self or the world's spirit. Over time, the will is moved to act upon them on the basis of this judgment. So, yes, we must humbly and honestly recognize the spiritual dimension of this inner struggle.

Remember St. Paul's testimony: "I fail to carry out the things I want to do, and I find myself doing the very things I hate." And such is his confident hope, because he knows "thanks be to God through Jesus Christ our Lord, we are rescued from this body…"

and we know that..."the Spirit too comes to help us in our weakness" (Romans 7-8).

God's spiritual direction is not always apparent to you or to your spiritual director. Especially when discernment centers on vocation in life and the deeper movements of prayer, the search can be quite prolonged and intricate. It takes time for it to be born into consciousness.

Be brave of heart: "At first, Wisdom may take us through winding ways, bringing fear and faintness upon us, plaguing us with her discipline until she can trust us. Wisdom tests with her ordeals. But in the end she will lead us back to the straight road and reveal her secrets to us" (Sirach 4:16-18). Contemplative souls, praying and listening deeply, come to recognize soul stirrings throughout their daily lives.

Now... we come to the most important awareness in any discernment process. What is God's answer to our specific question? We have prepared our hearts over time to seek the truth and to be as free as possible in accepting whatever response God wants for us in any given situation. We are seeking either a YES answer or a NO answer. We simply pay attention to those deep stirrings in our heart. Spiritual consolations indicate a YES answer and spiritual desolations indicate a NO answer to our discernment question.

Spiritual consolation

- Consolation is an experience of the soul being so on fire with God's love that we feel impelled to praise, love, and serve God and help others as best we can.

- There is courage, strength, peace, humility, light and goodness.

- Spiritual consolation encourages and facilitates a deep sense of gratitude for God's faithfulness, mercy, and companionship in our life.

- In consolation, we feel more alive and connected to others.

- Sometimes, we experience an inward burning love and tears of joy.

When you begin to detect <u>any</u> of these feelings and movements that leave you with a "spiritual consolation"…and these keep recurring throughout your process…then you can proceed with your discerned direction.

You are receiving a YES to your discernment question.

Spiritual desolation

- Desolation is an experience of the soul in disturbance and turmoil.

- There is a stirring up of anxiety, false sadness, needless confusion, frustration, and other obstacles.

- One can experience all sorts of troublesome thoughts and agitation, temptations, and be mired in self-preoccupations.

- We grow excessively restless and impatient and feel cut off from others.

- The focus is on earthly things and pleasures.

- Desolation stirs up discouragement, a loss of peace.

When you begin to detect <u>any</u> of these feelings and movements that leave you with a "spiritual desolation"… and these keep recurring throughout your process … then you can simply let the feelings and thoughts come and let them go.

You are receiving a NO to your discernment question.

<u>Do not mull over these feelings</u> as they can take you into a tail spin! Simply, let your discernment question go for now. In time, you may revisit the same question OR a new question. This NO can be helpful in keeping us on track and moving in harmony with God's direction. It also releases the psychological and physical tension of holding a question - indecision - over a long period of time. Let it go for now. Do not try to 'force' a discernment question into a YES answer. Sometimes God uses a NO discernment response to open up a new question. Often, something larger and wiser is being revealed.

With time and consistent practice using this contemplative discernment process, most persons usually find this simple YES or NO interior response as recognizable and trustworthy in making faith-based decisions.

The key question in interpreting spiritual consolation and spiritual desolation is: Where is the movement coming from and where is it leading me? Spiritual consolation does not always mean happiness. Spiritual desolation does not always mean sadness. Discernment is more intricate. Sometimes an experience of sadness is a moment of conversion and intimacy with God. It leads to tears of joy and felt mercy and a renewal of life. Times of human suffering can be moments of great grace as God's nearness comforts us in our letting go and surrender. Similarly, peace or happiness can be illusory if these feelings are helping us avoid changes we need to make. Is it a peace at any price?

For people who are trying to live a life pleasing to God, the Holy Spirit comes to strengthen, encourage, console, remove obstacles, and give peace. Discernment of spirits is a challenging task. It requires maturity, inner quiet, and an ability to reflect on one's interior life. We must be ready to improvise and adjust because God works in each of us so uniquely and depending on what stage we are at along the journey of life. It is recommended that we seek the assistance of a spiritual director in undertaking discernment of our major decisions.

A spiritual director will:
- Listen to you and help you name and identify the interior stirrings.
- Help you frame your question and check for inner resonance.
- Ask you further questions for reflection and prayer.
- Journey with you in listening to God's will in confident trust.
- Help you discern the fruits of the Spirit at work.
- Offer confirmation: seven signs that a spiritual direction has emerged.

"Now instead of the spirit of the world, we have received the Spirit that comes from God, to teach us to understand the gifts that he has given us."
- 1 Corinthians 2:12

Serious disciples cherish this discernment gift and put it to good use. Scriptures speak of the gift of discernment.

From the Hebrew Scriptures

Psalm 5: 1-3   Yahweh, let my words come to your ears, spare a thought for my sighs. Listen to my cry for help, my King and my God! I say this prayer to you, Yahweh, for at daybreak you listen for my voice; and at dawn I hold myself in readiness for you, I watch for you.

Deut. 30: 19 -20   I set before you life or death, blessing or curse. Choose life, then, so that you and your descendants may live in the love of the Lord your God, obeying his voice, clinging to him; for in this your life consists.

Psalm 85: 8-9   I am listening. What is Yahweh saying? What God is saying means peace for his people, for his friends, if only they renounce their folly; for those who fear him, his saving help is near, and the glory will then live in our country.

Isaiah 50: 4   Each morning he wakes me to hear, to listen like a disciple. The Lord Yahweh has opened my ear. For my part, I made no resistance, neither did I turn away.

Proverbs 15:14   The heart of the discerning makes knowledge its search, the mouth of fools feeds on folly.

Proverbs 3:5-6   Trust wholeheartedly in Yahweh, put no faith in your own perception; in every course you take, have him in mind: he will see that your paths are smooth.

Proverbs 1:5-6   Let the wise listen and he will learn yet more, and the man/woman of discernment will acquire the art of guidance. The fear of Yahweh is the beginning of knowledge; fools spurn wisdom and discipline.

From the New Testament Scriptures

Romans 12: 2   Do not model yourselves on the behavior of the world around you, but let your behavior change, modeled by your new mind. This is the only way to discover the will of God and know what is good, what it is that God wants, what is the perfect thing to do.

Phil. 1:9-11   My prayer is that your love for each other may increase more and more and never stop improving your knowledge and deepening your perception so that you can always recognize what is best. This will help you to become pure and blameless, and prepare you for the Day of Christ, when you will reach the perfect goodness which Christ Jesus produces in us for the glory and praise of God.

1 Cor. 12: 4-10   There is a variety of gifts but always the same Spirit; there are all sorts of service to be done, but always to the same Lord; working in all sorts of different ways in different

people, it is the same God who is working in all of them. The particular way in which the Spirit is given to each person is for a good purpose. One may have the gift of preaching with wisdom... another the gift of recognizing spirits...

Hebrews 5:14 Truly, anyone who is still living on milk cannot digest the doctrine of righteousness because he/she is still a baby. Solid food is for mature men/women with minds trained by practice to distinguish between good and bad.

1 Cor. 2:14-16   We teach spiritual things spiritually. An unspiritual person is one who does not accept anything of the Spirit of God: he sees it all as nonsense; it is beyond his understanding because it can only be understood by means of the Spirit. A spiritual man, on the other hand, is able to judge the value of everything, and his own value is not judged by other men.

1 Cor. 2:10   These are the very things that God has revealed to us through the Spirit, for the Spirit reaches to the depths of everything, even the depths of God.

Pause and Reflect

Reflect on your experience of praying with your discernment question.

Did you receive any locutions? These are words spoken from within the soul that just arrive when God wishes to communicate directly to a person. Sometimes they come in prayer, sometimes out of the blue. They just arrive, as we say!

How has talking about your discernment question with your spiritual director or pastor helped you come to a better understanding of this process of discernment?

Chapter 4

CONFIRMING THE DIRECTION

"Whether you turn to right or left, your ears will hear these
words behind you, "This is the way, follow it."
- Isaiah 30:21

As you pray with your question over time, gradually you'll begin to experience a consistent drawing towards a certain direction. As you contemplate following that direction, or even take the first steps toward following it, you will experience the fruits of the Spirit: courage, peace, joy, humility, strength, consolation. The prophet Jeremiah poured out his heart in this beautiful 'confession' as he yielded to God's alluring call: "You have seduced me Yahweh, and I have let myself be seduced; you have overpowered me: you were the stronger…Then there seemed to be a fire burning in my heart, imprisoned in my bones. The effort to restrain it wearied me, I could not bear it" (Jer. 20:7-9).

How do we know when we are being led by the Spirit of God? **There are 7 "signs"** that we can read in faith that act as criteria of good discernment.

1. Consistent recurrence
After lengthy discernment there is a consistent drawing towards a certain direction. The person then follows it. The further they go, the more they experience a mysterious inability not to pursue it. This "unable to be/to do otherwise" (Thomas Aquinas) is a compelling sign of authenticity. There will be a time of clarity which comes with undeviating persistence.

- What have been your inner urgent leanings?

- For how long have you noticed this sense of being called in this direction?
- Is there a strong feeling/attraction towards the direction you are praying with?
- Describe your experience of clarity and "being unable to do otherwise."

2. Continuity and discontinuity

The person recognizes that the new direction is a prolongation of their spiritual journey. Your spiritual genesis always had an innate thrust in this direction. At the same time, there is something new, a rupture, a leaving 'something' behind. The person must discontinue something in order to pursue following the emerging spiritual direction.

- Acknowledge your endings. Recognize that 'something' is shutting down. For example, there is no more energy or attraction for my present job, but I need the income. What could this be saying to me? How can God be in this ending? What would a new beginning look like for you? Be open and listen.
- An example of this might be a strong sense of call that one is to leave their secure job and start their own business. In time, they find themselves involved in a new career that is more suited to their personality and creativity. All their gifts continue to be shared. Another person might experience a call to leave her/his nursing career in a hospital setting only

to be led in time towards a ministry of spiritual healing and pastoral companionship in a different venue. God has wonderful ways of fulfilling our dreams and highest aspirations.

- Are you experiencing any of these shifts in your life right now?

3. Confirmation by others

After careful discernment, agreement among yourself and your spiritual director and your legitimate authority (e.g. your superior or community in the case of a religious; your spouse or family in the case of married persons) is a strong indication that a given direction is really from God.

If instead there is disagreement among the parties involved, one should continue the discernment and not embark upon the new direction immediately. Obedience is necessary here. More time or data may be necessary before there can be a confirmation of the direction by others.

- Tell your discernment question to your spouse, superior, pastor or spiritual director. Something happens when you 'tell' another trusted person what you have been undergoing for a considerable period of time.
- They may 'get it' right away and agree with your discerned decision. Or, they may need more time to reflect upon it, ask you some questions, and then consider it in their prayer time

privately. This is a good caution and helps with the confirmation signs.

Sometimes more data or discussion is needed so the other party can honestly look at your discerned decision and respond to you at a later date.

- How has this seeking confirmation by others been practical and useful in your experience?
- What are you coming to understand about how the Spirit works within your family, your community or workplace?

4. Peace

In following a particular direction, you will experience a "peace that the world cannot give" (Jn. 14:27). If the direction is truly from God, you will experience this deep peace accompanied by the undeniable conviction that to be true to God and to oneself, one cannot do other than proceed voluntarily in the direction indicated. Since it is so deep, this peace may coexist with considerable anxiety, hesitancy, uncertainty and fear of the unknown. While this may sound contradictory, it isn't! What may be perplexing to beginners in spiritual discernment is later embraced as a most profound grace.

- Can you describe your experience of this peace surpassing understanding?
- Ponder Mary at the moment of the Annunciation and her "How can this be?" followed by her beautiful surrender

prayer of "Let what you have said be done to me" (Lk 1:26-38).

This moment of grace calls for a YES that can sometimes contradict logic and reason. That is why one must stay the course. Resist the urge to have your rational and logical mind fully comprehend the new direction God seems to be calling you toward. "Acquiesce in the unknown and peacefully advance where you do not see the way" was a wisdom Thomas Merton experienced and validated in his critical choices. Faith is a trustworthy light upon our path.

5. The fruits of the Spirit

When a discerned direction is the work of some self-indulgence - 'just what I want to do' - the results are strife, rivalries, sexual irresponsibility, and resentment. When a discerned direction is the work of the Holy Spirit, the fruits are present: "What the Spirit brings is very different: love, peace, patience, kindness, goodness, trustfulness, gentleness and self-control" (Gal. 5:22). This 'sign' is extremely important because it confirms that the new direction is coming from God. The fruits of the Spirit cannot be self-created. This kind of intuitive 'knowing' within you further authenticates that the direction is coming from God.

- Do you recognize the 'particular way' the Holy Spirit works with you?

- What fruits have you been experiencing as you consider following the persistent nudging of your discernment question?
- Are they consistently present?
- Can you identify their stirring within you while in prayer and throughout the day?

6. Continued questioning

While you experience a deep conviction that you must follow the direction indicated, you may also experience continued questioning. We do not need to rationalize away every question or reservation that is expressed by others. Nor do we need to proudly claim absolute certainty. It is always with an attitude of humble faith and openness to receive further direction that one proceeds. True direction, while filled with the peace of Christ, in no way envelops us in clarity, security and precision.

Part of a discernment process is to examine oneself and face oneself with honesty and humility. This quiet and gentle admission that comes from such knowledge of self can be a helpful reminder that there is always a possibility that there may still be some selfishness involved. There is no need for self-righteousness or arrogance in our moving forward in faith.

- Can you speak to the 'kind of knowing' that comes from within when you say, "I believe God has called me to do this. I keep getting a strong sense that this is the direction."

Truly, this contemplative discernment process facilitates this inner knowing and gives a faith clarity that is a wonderful gift and brings such consolation and peace...even with all that remains unknown about the future direction.

- Can you recognize this openness to the Spirit growing in you?

7. Perseverance in living one's spiritual direction

Ultimately the authenticity of any direction is proven over time by one's living it out. This demonstrates that God is sustaining and upholding the person. It is not possible to sustain by one's will power alone. It is a God-given ability enabling one to fulfil what God sends one forth to do. Perseverance is then a sign of God's loving presence upholding and sustaining one by his abiding power and strength. "Never try to suppress the Spirit...think before you do anything...hold on to what is good" (1Thes. 5:19-22).

The full meaning and more ultimate implications of our new direction may only be revealed over time.

Reflect on your own experience thus far. A discernment process involves paying attention to 'the something new' that has been trying to break through into your awareness. Often, there is a lot of push and pull, sifting and sorting through what's coming from our emotional needs, our physical needs and our spiritual needs. Usually, that intensity has spanned over a period of time, for the big decisions anyway.

Over time, once one has acted in the new direction, God further confirms our YES by giving us perseverance in living out that new direction. We are gratefully sustained in the life that ensues from that decision. Even when new difficulties or trials come along, the core discernment remains steadfast and grace is supplied to help us stay the course.

- Journal an experience when this perseverance has manifested in your life. Possibly in your marriage or workplace relationships. Marvel at God's grace at work.

Pause and Reflect

All discernment has a beginning, middle and an end. It is a process. Where are you now? You might wish to share again with your spiritual director any of these new insights of the movement within your discernment process.

Usually, over time, a discernment direction is just there… with the accompanying 'signs' that this is the direction the Spirit is calling you to move in at this time. Name the direction you have discerned to handle your surface problem.

Live with it for a while before acting on it. Is there interior peace, recurring consistency, obedience and deeper faith and trust in God?

Chapter 5

FURTHER CLARITY

"You will be able to tell them by their fruits."
- Matthew 7:16

There are also personal, moral signs that one is being led by the Spirit

- Authenticity begets goodness, purity, love, humility. A morally good and loving person is a 'sign' of the presence of the Spirit. The person is God-directed, God-centred with a passion to do God's will.
- Increased love for God and others is always a constant 'sign' of the Spirit. Eventually the inward love of God shows itself in actions.
- A willingness to face persecution and suffering for Christ's sake is a true mark of the Spirit's presence. Trials strip the ego and make perfect love grow.
- Frugality marks the authentic person. One is content with necessities and the love of money is not present. Cares of the world can stifle the word of God.
- Uncluttered freedom in persons of the Spirit - inner detachment frees them for the things of the Spirit.

There are doctrinal signs that one is being led by the Spirit

- One speaks and practises sound doctrine, true to the Gospel. So many remain indifferent to the Gospel, or reject it outright. Some want a simple, sugar-coated pleasant version to make their life easier.

- God, "who so loves this world," commissions us to love one another with compassion, mercy and forgiveness.
- The message of the Gospel will not always be favourable with the majority. "If the world hates you, remember that it hated me before you. If you belonged to the world, the world would love you as its own; but because you do not belong to the world, because my choice withdrew you from the world, therefore the world hates you" (John 15-17). Our new 'direction' may result in hostility, rejection, the cold shoulder!
- A true prophet, speaking a 'word of God' for the correction/consolation/restoration of a community needs to be welcomed, not rejected. Prophetic ministries in the church are rigorously assessed and prophecies are vigorously tested. The Spirit opens the mouth of a true prophet to shake up and invoke reform and new life. "Now, I am making the whole of creation new" (Rev. 21: 5).

There are communal signs that one is being led by the Spirit

Unity: The ideal of unity is always humanly impossible. Therefore, it has always been a 'sign' of remarkable presence of the Spirit operative within the individuals who make up the community. Only the Spirit can create unity within a community and therefore, any action of the Spirit will not break the unity of the community. God speaks to an individual for the sake of the community. "May they all be one, Father, may they be one in us, as you are in me and I am in you, so that the world may believe it was you who sent me. I have given them the glory you gave to me, that they may be one as we are one" (Jn. 17:21-22).

The New Testament speaks of a healthy "diversity of gifts" within the community. There is no room for factions, dissensions and rivalries. These are not led by the Holy Spirit. The different gifts are given to different personalities to edify, exhort, console, and lead the community. They bring forth good effects and manifest in different ministries that build up the Mystical Body. The community must "never try to suppress the Spirit or treat the gift of prophecy with contempt: think before you do anything - hold on to what is good and avoid every form of evil" (1Thes. 5:19-22).

Obedience: Obedience freely given is a 'sign' of the Spirit's presence. God wills that his representatives be obeyed - not because they are wiser, better, more experienced - just because they are participants in the divine authority by the grace of their office. The pastor/minister or congregational leader does not have a direct pipeline to the Holy Spirit. They have to be converted and inwardly good so that the word of God can penetrate into their minds and hearts also.

John of the Cross, a Spanish mystic, wrote: "I do not want the soul to believe only by itself the communication it thinks are of divine origin, nor that anyone be assured or confirmed in them without the Church or her minister's confirmation." This obedience is a healthy safeguard in good discernment, especially in matters of making important decisions.

Pray with this Scripture

"My ways are not your ways, it is Yahweh who speaks. Yes, the heavens are as high above the earth as my ways are above your ways, my thoughts above your thoughts. Yes, as the rain and the snow come down from the heavens and do not return without watering the earth, making it yield and giving growth to provide seed for the sower and bread for the eating, so THE WORD that goes from my mouth does not return to me empty, without carrying out my will and succeeding in what it was sent to do" (Is. 55: 9-11).

Our deepest hope and desire is that our readers may come to enjoy the fullness of this gift of discernment. The ultimate goal is that discernment becomes a way of life. It can become a permanent attitude of listening to the interior voice of the Spirit. So freeing, so liberating, so joyous!

Some persons already live in an attitude of continuous attentiveness to the movements of the Spirit. This is called a contemplative lifestyle; living with 'a listening heart' in the daily ordinariness of life. It is a calm, gentle and receptive openness and mindfulness in the moment. YOU can begin to foster this desire within yourself by becoming more aware of the uniqueness of the Spirit's "still, small voice." Like Elijah at the door of the cave, we too start to recognize the Presence: "And after the fire, there came the sound of a gentle breeze" (1 Kings 19:13). We encourage you to practise this attentiveness in prayer and take time for reflection on specific life situations as they arise. Be mindful. Observe, without judgment. How is God nudging you towards 'the more?' What is 'the more' for you today?

It's really all about love. Discernment is ultimately about love. It is about seeing more clearly in the moment, the loving and compassionate action that is mine to choose and then having the freedom to respond and to act with grace.

It's total receptivity to God. As we come to live more and more in our true selves and in that place of our true identity, we are grasped by this Great Lover God. The habit of discernment is about coming to live in oneness with both God's desire and our deepest desire. That LOVE determines all our choices.

> "Give your servant a listening heart
> so as to be able to discern."
> -1 Kings 3:10

CONCLUSION

As we conclude our reflections on discernment, we do so confident of God's gracious love for us, securing and guiding us through all the stages of our spiritual journey.

Hopefully, you will be able to say YES to God and be more aware of the inner voice calling you each step along the way. "Pause awhile and know that I am God" (Ps 46:10). And "know that I am with YOU always; yes, to the end of time" (Mt. 28:20).

We are confident of this, "that the One who began this good work in you will see that it is finished when the day of Christ Jesus comes" (Philippians 1:6).

And to strengthen your hope, we profess that "it is God for his own loving purpose, who puts both the will and the action into you" (Philippians 2:13).

Pause and Reflect

Continue to practice this CONTEMPLATIVE discernment process. Describe your growing relationship with God.

How has your enhanced self-knowledge gifted you with living in more freedom, peace and joy?

CREDITS

de Chardin, Pierre Teilhard, S.J. Hearts on Fire, Praying with Jesuits. Edited by Michael Harter, SJ. The Institute of Jesuit Sources, St. Louis, 1993.

Medaille, Jean-Pierre, S.J. Writings of Jean-Pierre Medaille, SJ. Edited by Sisters of St. Joseph, Toronto, 1985.

Nemeck, Francis Kelly and Coombs, Marie Theresa. The Way of Spiritual Direction, Michael Glazier Inc., Wilmington, Delaware, 1985.

The Jerusalem Bible, Reader's Edition, Doubleday and Co., New York, 1971.

Personal Reflections…

A Future Full of Hope Series

Discernment: A Way of Life

The Mystery of Divine Indwelling

Dying Well

Understanding False Self and True Self

The Spirituality of the Paschal Mystery

The 8-fold Path of a Spiritual Life

Infinitely More…The Dark Night and Contemplation

Mary: A Contemplative Woman

The Spiritual Journey

Prayer: Remain in My Love

Manifestation of the Heart

The Eucharist: A Miracle of Love

Stages of Faith

The Spirituality of the Beatitudes

Going Deeper: The Mystical Way